HOW TO SAVE MONEY:

*25 Step-by-Step Tips
on How to Save Money by Cutting
Unnecessary Expenses Without
Sacrificing the Quality of Your Life*

Saving money is to do without something you want intensely, with the prospect that tomorrow you could wish something that probably you won't need.

Anthony Hope

ABOUT MONEY MASTERY TEACHER

The **Money Mastery Teacher** is a group of seasoned financial experts and an editorial team who understand and have infallible proves of the principles and application of economics and investment.

Through our work and 12+ years of professional experience as a financial advisor and business consultant for individuals, startups and existing businesses, **Money Mastery Teacher** now helps its audience and readers to make better financial decisions to improve their lives. We have published various topics covering a wide range of business and economics categories; from basics to advanced topics – including domestic economy and advanced investment solutions.

Money Mastery Teacher focuses on caring for an assortment of clients with regard to the development and growth of their individual investment strategies and business plans.

Very early on in our journey, **Money Mastery Teacher's** team members developed an enthusiastic interest in the world of capital markets and were able to acquire sound capital market knowledge through further educational pursuits.

Over the years, we have been aspired to provide objective and needs-based investment recommendations.

Our experience of just under 15 years in investment highlights the following:

"If your previous advisors have facilitated a bad rather than a better solution, then it was because they did not know better (lacking professional qualifications) or they lacked foresight and were bound inside-the-box to 'routine' corporate specifications."

Our Goal is to become your trusted investment advisory service through each chapter of our books – taking you by the hands and showing you how to engage proven business principles such as an open product selection, transparent pricing, and brand strategy, etc. – as you become a better player in your industry.

Through the various topics that are covered in our books, **Money Mastery Teacher** offers you a clever alternative to the traditional economy, investment strategy, and asset management. We believe that by working together with a specialized financial partner, you can achieve more.

With an understanding of the fact that every collaboration starts with a first conversation, **Money Mastery Teacher** is passionate about conversing with you through our books. Thus empowering you to become a better domestic economist or corporate investor.

We are always excited about the impact of the knowledge that we share with our readers – with respect to the added value created. Begin **Your Financial Freedom**, Today!!

INDEX

Reader's Guide 7

Brief references to minimalism 10

Organizing your expenses 14

1. Save 10% of your salary 19

2. Keeping fit autonomously without signing up to gym 21

3. One less coffee per day 26

4. Fighting your vice: quit smoking or smoke less .. 29

5. Moving with public or ecologic transport 34

6. Save your money on food shopping 38

7. Taking care of yourself in a healthy and economic way 42

8. Save money on your Bank Account 51

9. Save money on your free time 54

10. Save money on holiday 57

11. Bring lunch from home to the office 61

12. Choose generic drugs instead of original ones 64

13. Avoid gambling 68

14. Save money by Shopping Online 71

15. Save money by optimizing the use of household appliances 75

16. Use natural products to clean your home 80
17. Avoid disposable tableware 84
18. Save water and money 87
19. Save your money buying used school books 91
20. Save your money reading online newspapers .. 95
21. Save your money on Christmas presents 98
22. Grow food on your balcony or in an urban garden 102
23. Stop Ironing 107
24. Remove your landline 109
25. Save on light and gas bills, reading tips 112
Conclusion 120

Reader's Guide

Nowadays the whole world, small and large economic powers, is having bad days. The economic crisis has reached all commercial areas, all alliances and agreements between the various nations, which are increasingly trying to counter it without obtaining many results.

Italy is now on this distorted road for about ten years and the economic problem concerns everyone, translating itself into a sort of mass poverty. Taxes increase, work is scarce, raw material prices rise and it's all a domino effect, from which we try to escape trying to escape the domino that falls on us, in this case the problem that money is never enough. We are therefore all bound by the need to save for what today seems an uncertain future, or in any case to be able to go on each day with the most important expenses for us and for our family.

We know that money does not make happiness, but today not having them has become a real problem, once we lived with less and we were better, today we need an ever-increasing salary and it is difficult to save some money, even for just a mini-vacation or a small project. It is really the case to say that it was better when it was worse.

This small manual has been designed for those who have considered the idea of saving as much money as possible so that they can build a fund for a future, for a project, for emergency situations or to enjoy their retirement. It is a book that will address different aspects of life, if not all, and will allow the readers to reflect on their daily routine and on what they could do to improve it, while optimizing our lifestyle and our portfolio.

It is addressed to anyone, from an off-site student who must maintain himself, to those who have recently created their own individual reality and are trying to build something for the future, to those who are in financial difficulties and are looking for a solution, to those who have to support a family and look for a way to balance expenses. Each of us can have a motivation to improve his/her money management and save something, so the advice has been specifically written for every need.

A series of tips will be listed together with practical examples, to make the reader better aware of how much he will actually save, and not just in a theoretical way. The prices listed and the various situations have been based on reliable sources and through detailed research. In fact there will be hypertext links to be consulted if you are looking for further information.

This is just the first in a long series of manuals that will help you to save money and improve the organization of revenue of any type of consumer, thus creating a series dedicated to personal finance, hoping that given advices will help the readers to achieve their goals and make them more fulfilled and satisfied with their lives.

Enjoy your reading and have a good journey towards saving!

Brief references to minimalism

Since we are going to deal with money savings and management, let's take a look at what is called minimalism, a phenomenon to apply to everyday life exactly to save money. Let's not confuse it with the architectural style.

Minimalism is based on essentiality, on removing the superfluous and on the research for maximum enjoyment. Applying these principles to our lives will teach us to let go of what we don't need, to give the right value to things for the development of non-attachment and to create the right space in our life.

Why do we buy an item? We may not really need it, but we are attracted to something. A first step to adopt a minimalist lifestyle is to understand what we really need, the essential things, the ones we can't do without. So, if we have an impulse to buy things, then it would be good to start to think before buying them. But every once in a while it is also right to listen to the child inside us and give us a gift, make an exception to the rule, basically we are human.

Let's try to focus on just one single thing, in order to eliminate distractions, the superfluous. This also applies to non-material things, to be minimalist, you must be also when you do not make purchases. Eliminating distractions allows us to gain concentration and leads to excellent results. As we would also say later, quality is more important than quantity for a minimalist. It is not important to do a thousand things in life but to do it well, which is the same argument that applies when we buy groceries at the supermarket and the products are poor, but we buy them because they cost less. As we will see, it is possible to do quality shopping without exaggerating the waste of money.

In our life we will always meet someone with a more beautiful car, a more beautiful house, the latest mobile phone, but one of the rules of the minimalist style is precisely to look at our own garden. There are people in our world who can be happy even in dramatic conditions. If we succeed in achieving our goals and our victories, we don't need to envy others.

Eliminating what is superfluous does not mean eliminating everything we have, it means keeping what we like and it is really useful. For example our clothes, we can eliminate even more than half, to make space, take them to flea markets or give them to charity. However, there are still those we really need.

Minimalism, as we can see, can be used in all areas of our lives, including furnishing our home, for example. Having many paintings hanging on the wall is of no use, we would have nothing from that wall. If instead on that wall we had a photograph of a beautiful memory, every time we look at it will make us happy.

Another help that this life style can give us is precisely to teach us to organize ourselves and to maintain order in our home and in our lives, as well as into the wallet. Throwing away useless things, maintaining what is necessary and saving money makes our mind more tidy, together with our home and our life. Recycling, selling or donating items should not make us feel guilty. A garment removed from our closet can make someone else happy, for example, and remember that to surround ourselves with objects, especially if they are not ours, suffocate us.

Reading this manual we could realize what is really essential in our lives and what things are instead superfluous. Often we do not realize this because we do not analyze the situation carefully, but we will see how to learn from every area of our life.

Finally, wealth is not the most important thing in life, so we should be grateful for what we have, what we get from life and from what surrounds us. Gratitude is one of the bases of minimalism and helps us to reach our goals, ending up to be grateful to ourselves and to the change we make in our lives.

Organizing your expenses

Before starting with the advices on possible everyday situations, there is one very important thing to do to start our journey towards saving and improving our Money Management, which is an in-depth analysis of our total assets.

Depending on the personal situation, everyone has income coming from different directions and by analyzing them we could all understand what is our financial situation.

So the first step towards what will be our success is to sit at a desk, take a pen and paper and analyze every source of income that is in our heritage. The list is important just not to forget anything, also because without a proper analysis of our economic situation we cannot know how much we are really going to set aside or save.

For example, the list should include these data:

- Bank account

- Postal account

- Savings bonds

- Shares and securities

- Prepaid cards

- Wallet

- Money scattered around the house

- Piggy bank

- Any valuables things you would like to sell

- PayPal account

- Other money

- Investments

Some people would think they do not have all this heritage available, but maybe there is something that is taken for granted and not taken into consideration; it is better to realize exactly what we have before throwing ourselves headlong into our mission, because otherwise we will not have a real situation of what our economic condition is.

After making this accurate list the situation should be clearer and you can proceed to the second step, that is the "**Balance of your expenses**". Yes, because without an idea of the expenses that you actually deal with in everyday life, it is not clear how much money will be saved once the recommendations listed in the following pages are followed.

A useful and practical way to make an exact balance of the expenses could be to use an Excel table, filling rows and columns for the money spent and for the reason why we spent it. Or, if you are traditionalists, you can simply use pen and paper for the same organizational work. To make an exact balance of our expenses, it is useful to keep the receipts of all the purchases we make, for example in a month, and then bring them back to the table or list we are going to write. With the receipts of the last month or more months, we will take into account the actual costs incurred.

Now, once our economic situation is clear, both in terms of revenue and expenditure, we can set the "**Savings target**" and the when we want to achieve it. Having a goal and striving to achieve it stimulates our mind to work better and consistently so that, having a fixed point, we head towards It. There will certainly be moments of discouragement, moments in which we will think of not making it but it is a bit like if it were a job.

At office, our boss wants us to achieve goals, which will be useful for us to reach a promotion or for the company to improve. At the university we have exams to pass to reach the degree. This "**Savings goal**" should be the fuel for our will, that will allow us to reach the goal and save the money that we have set for ourselves at the beginning of our challenge, or to have saved money from our wallet, to use them in other more pleasant purposes.

Anyway, to do this, you have to develop a plan. A "**Savings Plan**" will be used to understand how to set aside, how much and when. We could also consider adopting new habits that will allow our pockets to be fuller, such as paying cash and not with a credit card, so that we can physically account for the expense we are facing and the money we are actually paying, taking it away from our heritage; or separating the different current accounts, for example one for expenses and one for savings, in order to better manage the money. Another idea could be to reflect on the purchases to be made. To avoid impulsive purchases we could reflect 24h on what to do, to actually think if that particular object is really necessary or not. These are some of the tricks that will allow us to achieve our goal and to balance the accounts.

Also in this case, drawing up a table could be an excellent idea.

Finally, before starting to put into practice the list of recommendations contained in this manual, it is better to prepare a final table for each expense on which we will actually save money, to be filled in every time we set something aside.

Now, after this brief introduction to money saving and situation our ideas on our heritage are clearer, we can go on reading and following the advice below for a better return on our work.

1. Save 10% of your salary

The first advice to put in place should relate to our income and therefore our salary, or what gives us a living, for example a pension or another kind of income, since it is the money we are going to invest and spend during the month and year. Affecting our salary by immediately paying taxes and bills would lead us to have to sacrifice part of it immediately. If instead we put aside a small percentage of our salary as soon as it is paid into our account, this will allow us to save immediately, before facing other types of situations that we will see later.

An average salary in Italy is **€ 1500** net per month on average, therefore less than **€30,000** gross a year. Obviously this is an average calculation, which means that not everyone takes € 1500 a month, but only a part. In fact, those who work as clerks, workers or employees receive a much lower salary. We are the ninth country in Europe in terms of average salary, Spaniards do worse, in tenth place. The crisis has invaded all of Europe and even many other countries in the world, but Italy is one of those that has suffered it the most.

95% of people employed by private companies in Italy are classified as employees or workers. Only 1.4% are managers and 4.3% are executives, who receive a higher salary. Lombardy is the region with the highest salary, where the average salary is **€ 31,000** gross a year. Trentino and Liguria follow. The lowest salary is received in Sicily with about **€ 23,000** gross a year. There is a clear division between north and south, and this does not only apply to salaries but to general living conditions.

In Europe the situation is different, for example the lowest salaries are paid in eastern countries but at the same time these are countries in which companies, including Italian ones, go to invest. The country with the highest salaries is Denmark.

Receiving an average salary of **€ 1500**, we could save 10% of this at the exact moment when it is paid into our bank account, by doing so we could at least guarantee a small monthly saving that otherwise we would spend for something else, be it a whim or a bill. Picking up 10% and setting it aside we will already have a small nest egg to put in our piggy bank. 1500 * 10/100 = 150. Not bad to start our adventure in the world of savings.

THIS ADVICE WILL ALLOW YOU TO SAVE € 150 PER MONTH (€ 1800 YEARLY).

2. Keeping fit autonomously without signing up to gym

For each of us health should be placed first in our scale of values and needs of life. Keeping fit therefore should be one of our prerogatives. Given the importance of this aspect of our lives, we place physical activity as the first one of the long list of examples we're going to do.

We all signed up to the gym at least once in our lives for different reasons, but all linked by a single purpose, to keep fit, maybe for the summer to come.

Just the fact of enrolling in the gym, having paid a subscription even for a short time, often stimulates our mind to keep with our commitment not so much for our body, but often for our portfolio.

Thinking about the € 300 we spent on an annual gym membership triggers the input to go and train at least a couple of times a week and to not feel guilty about spending money. It is a purely psychological factor, we are all able to be constant in an activity even if we do not spend millions. We need only the will and a precise goal.

Without making a bundle of grass, we can say that

surely there are people who sign up the gym or other activities because they are determined to achieve a perfect shape in their eyes, to feel better, to take their mind off the stressful routine or simply to know new people.

Regardless of which of these reasons pushes a person to buy a gym membership, you can practice sports for free by adding just a little extra willpower.

As a first step you could draw up a list with the days in which to train and which exercises or activities you want to do.

For example, if you are a fan of running or, in the gym, you usually do Cardio, the perfect places for this type of activity are the promenade, a park, a pine forest, a cycle path, which are often equipped with tools suitable for those who do train, as parallel and traction bars. But you can also go home after a long run, lay a towel on the ground, do some stretching and then do push-ups, sit-ups, leg exercises, etc. Doing all these exercises costs nothing, if not a few hours of our time.

If, on the other hand, you are not us to practicing sports or you are afraid of not doing the exercises in the right way, you can take a brisk walk outside, doing only some simple exercises.

In case you don't love walking or running and you just want to devote yourself to exercises, you can set up a mini DIY gym with some of the items we already have at home. A towel on which to do the exercises, a broomstick to do squats, a stool in case you want to do step, belts of the bathrobe instead of elastic bands for stretching, a wall of the home for exercises in which you need support and much more, just a little imagination is enough and, on the base of one's needs, everyone could set up their sports space without too much difficulty.

Furthermore, it must be said that today the web offers a lot and it is easy to find video tutorials or personal trainers that explain the exercises in the best way and help to follow a satisfying sporting journey.

Even our smartphones could be of help, downloading from the stores some Apps that allow you to record the data of the completed sport activity, give suggestions for feeding and remind the user when there is the next training session. For iOs and Android there is Runkeeper, an app for runners created by Asics, Keep Training, in different versions, depending on the sports field you need, or MyFitnessPal, which helps you achieve goals such as weight loss.

Finally, another activity you can do at home or

outdoors, using a tutorial or an app, is yoga, famous and known by everyone activity. It is a complete activity that manages to balance body and mind at the same time leaving the wallet intact. To date, oriental disciplines are very popular in the West and it is increasingly common to see people who practice them and follow a routine according to ancient patterns, such as Ayurveda, of which the yoga discipline is part.

As regards clothing, you can use old and worn clothing that you no longer use as before.

The only minimum cost to afford could be the shoes, that can be found at low price. Shoes are important because if you walk badly or run incorrectly, you can have back problems, and the right shoes help.

So, a minimum subscription to the gym costs **€ 50** per month, adding **€ 40** for the medical certificate that you need to start the course and about **€ 20** for signing up, thus spending **€ 110** initially. Instead, by making an annual subscription, which can cost around € 300, the cost will be around **€ 360**.

Not enrolling in the gym but setting up a space at home with a minimum of equipment that includes dumbbells (on average **€ 10**), elastic bands (**€ 20**), exercise bikes (about **€ 100**), parallel bars (**€ 50**), you would spend about **€ 180**, which is half of the previous example.

Finally, by not enrolling in the gym and not buying any type of specific equipment, so practicing a sporting activity using the objects you have at home, or doing it in the open air, you would not spend anything. The advantage of giving up a gym membership is to stay in shape by putting aside some savings that can be used for a future project.

THIS SIMPLE ADVICE WILL ALLOW YOU TO SAVE FROM € 180 TO € 360.

3. One less coffee per day

Coffee is the most drunk drink in the world and it is something that we Italians hardly give up, in fact we consume about 5.9 kg a year, per person. Whether in the form of a cappuccino, a cup of coffee or a simple espresso, it is consumed daily, especially in the morning, before reaching the workplace. For many of us, having breakfast with coffee and a croissant is a sort of ritual, a moment of privacy, a preparation for the day, often stressful, that we must deal with.

But this little special moment of the day costs our wallet a little bit of change a month, with which we could get something more fulfilling and satisfying even for a distant future.

This advice is not intended to make you give up with your coffee ritual, but to change the way it is taken and to make you consider that we could get some benefits with this new habit. As in the previous example, you could avoid a place where you need to spend money to drink it, in this case the bar, and maybe enjoy a coffee, perhaps even better, at home, made with a classic mocha. A simple coffee at the bar costs on average € 1, taking us to spend about **€ 30** a month. In addition to coffee you often buy a croissant or a pastry, which on average costs **€ 1.50**, spending **€ 2.50** every morning for a total of **€ 75** per month.

We often do not realize how much our habits can cost, almost as much as a bill, or that we could use the same money for a future project, which is could be a journey we have been dreaming of for some time.

Setting aside **€ 1** or **€ 2.50** a day can give a lot of satisfaction at the end of a long collection period, and helps to motivate us to better achieve our goals, even if they seem light-years away. When that jar is filled with coins, which will be used for an important project, we will feel satisfied and proud of our success.

We will continue to drink our fragrant coffee in the morning, but doing it in a more economical way, preparing an espresso with mocha and some ground coffee.

A packet of ground coffee for mocha costs about **€ 3**, which is 3 coffees at the bar, so you can drink about 33 cups of coffee while staying at home and saving a lot of euros.

You would save, only on coffee, a hefty **€ 27** a month.

Often we are greedy and we also want our little sweet to make our day more enjoyable. But we could avoid buying it and making a donut, for example, with our hands, needing only eggs (**€ 1**), water, sugar (**€ 1**), flour (**€ 1**), baking powder (**€ 2**) and maybe chocolate (**€ 2**) to make breakfast sweeter, for a total of **€ 7** which could become something more if you take into account the time and electricity used. But a donut will stay in our house for a week, and considering the average weekly cost of **€ 10.50** for a croissant in the morning, we will save about **€ 3.50** a week, which in a month will become about **€ 14**.

So, coffee and a croissant every morning make us spend about **€ 44** a month, while doing the same thing at home we would spend **€ 31** a month. It's **€ 13** of difference, which could be saved for a bigger goal.

For example, with the money that you do not spent at the bar you could buy one of those machines with pods, which today are all the rage and are suitable for all the different needs and tastes of customers, as well as being affordable. Pods cost on average € 0.30 each, so about 3 coffees with that euro that is spent at the bar for just one coffee

You don't need to give up pampering or Zen moments before a stressful day, but you simply need to change the way you do it if you want to save some money.

THIS SIMPLE ADVICE WILL ALLOW YOU TO SAVE € 13 PER MONTH.

4. Fighting your vice: quit smoking or smoke less

Smoking kills! A typical phrase we find on cigarette, cigar and tobacco packages. Certainly it is certainly not good for our health, but it is a practice that has been going on for centuries. Worldwide, to date, there is about one billion people who smoke, certainly less than in 2016, and who create a very large business for large and small powers. Also the pollution factor should be noticed, due to the cigarette butts dispersed in the environment.

The average price of a pack of cigarettes is around € 5. An average smoker smokes about 13 cigarettes a day, which means that he spends about € 1200 a year and if the accounts are not wrong, its monthly costs about € 100.

This considering only the economic aspect, but what about the healthy aspect of the topic?

In fact, a smoker does not calculate the danger that his body runs by ingesting handfuls of smoke every day, he thinks that the problems related to this vice will occur in a remote future. But in reality our body immediately begins to manifest the diseases related to smoking, starting from the mouth, as it is in close contact with the cigarette itself. Tooth enamel weakens along with gums, which are more prone to diseases such as periodontitis, and finally the breath that will smell like smoke forever. Then there is the respiratory system, which in a short time is damaged making us exposed to serious diseases such as tumors. Finally, there is the skin, which is deprived of oxygen and becomes opaque due to smoking.

In short, only by reading these things we should realize that in addition to the wallet we would preserve also our health and that of those around us. Yes, even passive smoking is not good, especially for children or those suffering from respiratory problems.

Returning to the costs that a smoker bears every month, we must consider also the lighters. It is known that these are lost and left elsewhere continuously and this causes the smoker an expenditure of about **€ 5** monthly, considering that on average a lighter costs **€ 1**. Maybe **€ 5** a month seems nothing compared to what we spend for shopping, paying taxes and bills, but **€ 5** a month become **€ 60** a year and this already sounds different to our ears.

If health is not the first thought of a smoker, maybe his wallet is, so taking off the habit of smoking could contribute a lot to save money.

THIS COUNCIL WILL ALLOW YOU TO SAVE ABOUT € 105 PER MONTH.

If, on the other hand, you can't stop smoking, if your willpower is not strong enough and if the advice just suggested is not helpful, then we can also take another route, that of the famous handmade cigarettes, only if you are not too lazy.

A pack of loose tobacco containing 30g of product, costs on average **€ 6** and allows to make about 100 cigarettes, those that an average smoker would consume in about a week, thus spending **€ 24** a month compared to **€ 100** of cigarette packets. But remember that in addition to tobacco we also need filters and rolling paper, the former has a cost of **€ 1.50** per package containing 150 filters, while the rolling paper cost **€ 0.50** and each package has 50 inside.

So, an average smoker who consumes 390 cigarettes a month would need:

- 4 packs of loose tobacco for **€ 6** each (6 * 4 = 24)

- 3 packs of filters of 150 pieces at a cost of **€ 1.50** each (1.50 * 3 – 4.50)

- 7 packets of 50 pieces each one for **€ 0.50** each (0.50 * 7 = 3.50)

Thus having a total of **€ 32**, compared to **€ 100** for regular cigarette packages.

Loose tobacco certainly allows a lot of tobacco consumers to save money, who will create their own cigarettes, but never as much as the advice to completely stop smoking and take better care of your person.

THIS ADVICE WILL ALLOW YOU TO SAVE € 68 PER MONTH.

Finally, another way to continue smoking while saving money is the use of the electronic cigarette, which in addition to helping us with savings will help us stop smoking and therefore take care of our lungs.

Liquid for electronic cigarette has an average cost of **€ 5** per 10ml, which we will use for about two weeks, spending an average of **€ 10** a month. Consider that to start we will need a starter kit of about **€ 40**, including cigarette and liquid, the resistance of the cigarette is to be changed every three months and costs about **€ 5**. We will arrive at the end of the year spending **€ 180** including starter kits. Let us remember that buying normal cigarettes we would spend **€ 1200** a year.

The electronic cigarette is also a way to quit smoking

or otherwise reduce cigarette consumption. In addition to the money you can save, it's better for your lungs. Many people have found themselves better because the electronic cigarette, in addition to its good smell and to money saving, does not leave the throat dry, does not cause cough or phlegm to those who use it.

Quitting smoking would be certainly better, also because there are those who speak well of it but, like any merchandise on the market, there are those who believe that the electronic cigarette is more harmful than the traditional cigarette. But we know how things go, not everyone likes them. Here the question is about us and of our journey towards savings, so we have to choose the path we prefer.

THIS ADVICE WILL ALLOW US TO SAVE € 1020 PER YEAR.

5. Moving with public or ecologic transport

Every day we use car to move from one part of the city to another, whether it is to go to work, to accompany or take children back to school, go to the gym, go shopping or for many other reasons why we can't or won't go on foot.

We now know very well that our planet is in danger due to smog, plastic, global warming and much more, and using the car we are certainly not helping to make the situation better, and certainly we do not even improve the condition of our wallet.

One of the expenses that most affects the assets of a person and a family is that for car maintenance. The expenses related to the car insurance, the ownership tax, the maintenance and above all the fuel, mean that within a year you usually spend a lot money that could be saved for unpleasant situations or for your future retirement period.

Car <u>maintenance costs</u> reach an average of **€ 1500** per year. The expense with the higher impact on this sum is obviously the fuel, which covers a good 50%. These data are indicative because in any case there is a clear difference in costs between North and South Italy:

fuel prices vary from region to region, for example Molise is the region where filling up the car costs more than other regions such as Lazio, Sicily and Marche.

Here we are describing just the average consumption that a person can sustain for the maintenance of his/her car.

The periodical maintenance and the ownership tax carry 11% of the cost, which on average is **€ 171** per year. Everyone can then calculate exactly what is the cost of his/her car or cars. Because in fact it often happens that in a household there is more than one car, sometimes reaching up to three cars per household. It is not a coincidence that Italy is the country that owns more cars, followed by the United States.

This is certainly a blow to our pockets and also to the surrounding environment, as well as to our health.

It is possible to live without a car, there are many other means of transport available. Who lives in big cities like Milan, Turin or Naples, can use the underground, for which the monthly pass costs on average **€ 70**, for a total of **€ 840** per year. As regards a bus season tickets, it costs about **€ 40** per month, which would be € 480 at the end of the year.

Finally the most ecological solution, which is possible everywhere in our country, because fortunately we have a landscape suited to the situation together with fairly mild climate, it is the bicycle, especially when spring comes, when the days are warm and there is no more the risk of getting a sore throat. An average city bike costs **€ 390**.

Certainly everyone has his own needs and it is not always possible to permanently avoid the use of the car, but doing so the wallet would certainly have benefits.

If you use car only for small journeys, then the motivation to avoid it should increase, also because many things could be done on foot, and returning to the first advice, there would be no reason to sign up to the gym, you could go shopping , take the children back to school, go out with friends, using only your own legs. Consider that there are people who have to do it because they can't afford a car.

Looking at the environment, the air we breathe would improve a lot if each of us decided to eliminate at least one car per household. In Italy there are many cities that exceed smog levels continuously and this causes an exponential increase in diseases and allergies. Fortunately, we have not yet reached the levels of Thailand, but we should start to take some common sense about environment, it is still not too late to improve the situation.

A new recent entry on our roads is the Car Sharing service, or an alternative way to move around the city without spending a lot, sharing the same mean of transport. This new method of moving is useful if you have to do many kilometres and there is not the possibility of using other alternative means. If we all get used to car sharing, carbon dioxide emissions would halve. So even if the car is really necessary it is possible to share it, saving money and giving more oxygen to our lungs. One of the ways to use the Car Sharing service is BlaBlaCar.it, the site par excellence. But this new way of travelling can also be put into practice with colleagues or friends. For example, why not share petrol with one of our work colleagues?

By eliminating car and using public transport, bicycle or a Car Sharing service, you would save enough money for a good future project, for an investment that would lead to other revenues or a fund to be used tomorrow. And remember, we could help improve the environment.

THIS ADVICE WILL ALLOW YOU TO SAVE FROM € 660 TO € 1500 A YEAR

6. Save your money on food shopping

Grocery shopping, one of the most typical everyday situations for a person and perhaps one of those that we find easier to do. You go to the supermarket, take a cart and buy what you need. But it's not really that simple. Shopping sometimes also involves choices, especially today when the general economic situation is not the best and there is a tendency not to buy quality food or items thinking of saving money.

There are different ways to save money when shopping at the supermarket but often our hectic life makes us impatient and we tend to put our products in the cart without noticing what we really need. Simply, to save money you should pay attention to certain small things and change some habits.

To begin we should draw up a list of what we really need and on the base of what we eat. That is a list that allows you to buy what will be used to support our body without exaggerating in quantity.

The list helps us to follow a path, to keep ourselves firm from the temptation to go for a stroll through the supermarket, filling the cart with futile things, forgetting maybe what we really need.

Secondly, but not least, it is advisable to eat something before going shopping, as having an empty stomach would make us vulnerable to buying anything we see that teases our appetite. Spending on a full stomach is good for your health and your wallet. Having an empty stomach we will try to rob the supermarket for all the products we want at the moment and this can make us happy for a limited amount of time but it will affect our pockets extensively.

Each envelope from the fruit and vegetable sector costs on average **€ 0.02** and an envelope at the cash desk, to put all our expenses, **costs on average € 0.05**. In addition to our wallet, also the environment is affected. Why buy plastic bags, even if biodegradable, if we can use the same shopping bag every time? Cloth bags are cheap and allow us to save a lot on envelopes helping the environment. Returning to the minimalist lifestyle, buying plastic bags is really a waste for us and the environment.

Choosing the place to do our shopping is important because, if it is true that we are what we eat, we should choose the products we buy very carefully, for example buying them in a good supermarket or market that sells fresh and seasonal fruit and vegetables. Fruit and vegetables should be bought at the market, by farmers, so as to be sure of the quality of the products. The supermarket tends to have industrial products often full of chemicals

The discount store itself is not a bad idea to consider, it does not mean that if a supermarket sells at a lower price than another, its products are all poor. Many of the cheap discount products are excellent and sometimes even better than branded ones.

Speaking of prices, we have to keep an eye on the promotions we often find in supermarkets. Nowadays, every supermarket offers different offers, but be careful which ones are really convenient and which ones are not. Consider that promotions often serve to make the trolleys fill so it is good to pay attention. We must pay attention not only to the price, but also to the quantity of the product.

Furthermore, the best thing to do is to produce homemade goods such as bread, pasta and other delicacies that can contribute to our needs. It could also be a nice pastime or a way to challenge yourself in new activities. In order not to waste money we can use technology, for example downloading Apps such as My Flyer, which allows you to browse the supermarket flyers with available offers; or WhereisBetter that indicates the nearest shops with the best prices.

One last thing to do is to better organize our pantry. Apart from fresh products there are products such as canned vegetables, biscuits or pasta that have a long shelf life. By organizing the dispensation in the best way we would have a better perception of what our needs are. Even for milk we could opt for long-term packaging, perhaps making it a stock to save money and not buy it for a while.

An Italian family spends on food, according to Istat data, on average **€ 457**. But really how many of the things we buy actually serve? The essential products are: pasta (**€ 2**), rice (**€ 2**), milk (**€ 1** per liter), eggs (**€ 1**), fresh fish (**€ 15**), fresh meat (**€ 5** per pack), vegetables (**€ 5** on average per kg), fruit (**€ 3** on average per kg), cheese (**€ 5**), olive oil (**€ 5**) and spices (**€ 1**). Considering buying only these primary goods weekly, with the average prices listed, we would spend **€ 45**, for a total of **€ 180** monthly.

THIS ADVICE WILL ALLOW YOU TO SAVE ABOUT € 277 PER MONTH.

7. Taking care of yourself in a healthy and economic way

We all seek a way to please ourselves, looking for a way to take care of our image so that it is reflected in the mirror exactly as we want. We do not feel beautiful in several ways, we do not feel pleasant when we look at the image of our face or our body reflected in the mirror. So everyone in their own way tends to work on their physical appearance.

The reason that leads us to look the best is often given by society itself, by globalization, by the standards, and we are led to change our appearance with various and different practices. Sometimes, however, we simply take care of our body and our appearance to pamper ourselves and give us a moment of relax, a personal moment, in one of our reserved spaces, a sort of sancta sanctorum.

In the centuries that history tells us, physical embellishment has always been present, let's think for example of ancient Egypt where queens and pharaohs adorned their faces with natural substances that were the equivalent of our make-up, coloured nails with enamels and enjoyed baths in donkey's milk or steam, as for example in the famous thermal baths of ancient Rome. Even the deceased were embellished, washed, treated and made up to look their best in the presence of their gods.

The care of our body is therefore certainly something important, something that each of us does even minimally, whether it is to enjoy a day at the spa or a morning at the hairdresser.

In this advice those aspects of taking care of oneself, which are more usual in the day or in the life of an ordinary person, will be observed, in order to understand how to save money by continuing to pamper us.

To date it is no longer the case to make distinctions between women and men, as we all use more or less the same practices to cure our body. Maybe once it was only the woman who took care of herself in a more meticulous way, while today men, at times, almost tend to be more feminine than women themselves. Therefore the situations taken into consideration will be expressed for both genders.

Starting from the head, we usually tend to go to the hairdresser or the barber once a month. Consider first a hairdresser for women. A styling in Italian beauty salons costs on average **€ 18.50**, depending on the type of salon you go to and the skill of the hairdresser.

A haircut instead comes on average **€ 30**, including styling, although in some cases you can even get to **€ 40**. The hair dyeing, which inevitably needs to be done monthly, can cost an average **€ 50**, depending on which technique is chosen, mèches, balayage or other. So an Italian woman will spend about **€ 80** a month at the hairdresser.

And if instead we wanted to opt for a less expensive choice? There are many products that can be used at home, such as dyes and hair treatments, which can be purchased in supermarkets or special centres, and if you are brave enough you can also buy special utensils to brush, cut and thin your hair.

The initial kit to buy must be made up of a brush (**€ 10**), professional scissors (**€ 20**), often also containing a comb or a pair of extra scissors, scissors for thinning hair (**€ 10**), kit for dyeing composed of brush and small bowl (**€ 5**), disposable gloves (**€ 4**) and hair care products (**€ 20** on average). Spending initially about **€ 70**, for tools that will last for years and products that last for months, which is a cut with styling from the hairdresser.

Then as regards the hair dyeing we must consider that a package of hair dye costs on average **€ 5**, some of which also offer the kit with brush and gloves, shampoo and cream. This will be the only cost to be incurred monthly.

THIS ADVICE WILL ALLOW YOU TO SAVE FROM € 15 TO € 75 PER MONTH.

Nowadays even men show to really care about their look and in addition to devoting themselves to fitness and nutrition, they are often very demanding about their hairstyle and hair care, and some often even about their beard.

A man <u>in Italy</u> normally spends about **€ 20** per month to the barber shop only for the haircut, which sometimes is twice during the month, depending on the person and his needs. There are also those who love to dye their hair and for this they spend about **€ 30**, although even in this case, as for women, it depends on the technique used by the hairstylist and the hair must be dyed monthly because of the famous re-growth. Finally comes the beard treatment, which costs about **€ 15**, depending also on the products used in the case of famous hipster beards. So every month a man will spend around **€ 65** to embellish and take care of his beard and hair.

With those **€ 65** spent monthly, you could buy an electric shaving and hair shaving machine, but it will only have to be bought once. Even men could buy scissors (**€ 10**) or shaving brushes (**€ 10**) which often also includes a conditioner for it. It is also possible to buy beard care products (about **€ 25**). All this for a total of **€ 110** which, however, should no longer be spent.

The only monthly expense to do is that of the dye, at an average cost of **€ 10**, if needed, and shaving foam (**€ 2**).

THIS ADVICE WILL ALLOW YOU TO SAVE FROM € 50 TO € 63 TO MONTH.

Now, another interesting topic for both genres is facial treatment, from the appointment with the beautician to the daily creams, passing then to make-up.

Eyebrows, mustaches and other facial hair, are the classic thing to which, at least once a month, we have to dedicate an hour of our time going to the beautician, who will make us hurt but more appreciable to society and to ourselves.

An appointment for facial waxing by a beautician, in Italy, costs on average **€ 15**, while buying the wax and making it on your own will cost an average **€ 10** per pack, which we could reuse even for other delicate parts - usually the face, bikini area and underarms waxes are the same product.

Speaking about creams and facial treatments, using famous and expensive brands we will spend about **€ 50**, considering creams, masks and eye contour. Sometimes even if a product is expensive it is not really healthy for our body, like we said bout food at the supermarket. Some branded products, especially make-up, are full of chemicals and metals that damage our skin instead of making it more beautiful or fit. Furthermore a lot of people are allergic to nickel which is in 90% of the products we buy.

Many companies produce cosmetics and creams based on vegetables that absolutely do not harm our body, but it still would be better to prepare your own treatments, such as a scrub composed of honey, lemon and cane sugar, suitable for those who have an oily skin. Using ingredients that you have at home, such as fruit, sugar, baking soda, coffee, you have no expense but the one made at the supermarket to buy the food necessary for our needs.

Finally let's consider the make-up, for which we also can say "not because it costs a fortune then it is the best". There are so many companies that over the years and because of their fame now sell cosmetics at exorbitant prices, while others that cost less are better, as well as in the price and in the composition. For example, a YSL mascara can cost around **€ 40**, and is composed of nickel and other chemical materials that does not allow the skin to breathe, while a mascara composed of plant elements, such as those made by Yves Rocher, can cost **€ 16**. Let us not be deceived by the price that often does not mean "quality"[1].

For the rest of body we have to consider about the same things. Body treatments can cost up to about **€ 100**, and go to a beautician on a monthly basis to shave legs, arms and groin costs **€ 45** on average.

Home-made waxing would us to save a lot of money, considering that you can buy a pack of wax for around **€ 10**, while for the rest of the body products we could simply change the brand, raising the quality level. If we are really good we could also consider the idea of producing wax at home with kitchen ingredients, such as Arab wax, one of the best on the market is made with honey and sugar.

Let's consider then an adult woman who goes to the beautician every month to depilate her whole body,

---

[1] The mentioned brands are just an example of what we can find on the market

uses products for body care and uses non-vegetable make up, but normal cosmetics. The cost of full treatment at the beauty centre will cost around **€ 60** (**€ 45** for body and **€ 15** for face), the monthly cost for body care products reaches a cost of **€ 100** (body moisturizer, scrub, hand cream, exfoliating) and that for face care reaches a cost of **€ 50** (toning, cleansing milk, face cream, make-up remover). Finally, make-up will cost about **€ 100** (pencil, mascara, lipstick, foundation and concealer for dark circles). All these products and treatments will steal from our pockets **€ 310**.

If the same woman wanted to save money, she could buy cheaper products and cosmetics, paying about **€ 100** for both creams and make-up. In addition, she could prepare some DIY wax for just **€ 10**.

THIS ADVICE WILL ALLOW WOMENS TO SAVE OF ABOUT € 200 PER MONTH.

Now let's consider an average man who monthly goes to the beautician for a facial treatment (**€ 10** without considering moustaches) and body (**€ 45**), buys products for the face such as moisturizing cream, exfoliating cream and eye contour, spending about **€ 50**, reaching a total of **€ 110**. If the same man decides to change the products he uses, spending up to **€ 30** and shaving with a razor that costs **€ 15**, using tweezers for his eyebrows **(€ 3** only once), his pockets would have a great benefit.

THIS ADVICE WILL ALLOW MEN TO SAVE € 60 PER MONTH.

8. Save money on your Bank Account

Another way to save money is to check our bank account, because it, like so many other things, has its costs. Every bank has its offers, its types of saving programs, but sometimes there are expenses that we don't calculate in our budget and we should pay attention to. So another advice is to check the expenses of our bank account and inform about what we can reduce, or to investigate to change type or bank, on the base on market offers.

For example we can control how much our credit card costs annually, constantly check the conditions that the bank proposes to those who have our type of bank account and start using the ATM instead of a credit card to avoid unnecessary fees. We could then use the bank's online service, making bank transfers from home or other types of transactions, so that the service does not have the cost that would have at bank. Finally, instead of withdrawing anywhere it would be better to get cash from our bank ATMs so as not to run into exaggerated commissions, paying to withdraw our money and affecting our savings.

Saving on the bank account, therefore, can be

something not to be overlooked because often bank commissions are high, and greatly reduces our assets in the long run. The home banking service is becoming increasingly popular and the banks are trying to adapt by making online services available at a much lower cost than they usually have in their physical structure. There are several economic plans to open a bank account online instead of that we currently use, saving money. This should however be done carefully, without the risk of possible scams with websites that we do not know. We should try to turn to banks whose background we know well.

There are free online accounts, which means that you have not to pay when you open it, and that are exempted from monthly fees, but let's remember that this type of account allows free transactions only online, while you have instead to pay at the counter. However in this case you would have available credit and debit cards. Considering that the average annual amount of a bank account in Italy is **€ 80**, opening an online account will allow you to save your money.

THIS ADVICE WILL ALLOW YOU TO SAVE ABOUT € 80 PER YEAR.

If you are not used to the Internet, instead, there are many ready-to-use solutions. These packages provide a monthly fee but give access to many banking and extra banking operations. The savings will be less than an online bank account, but it is better than nothing. Usually these services cost an average of **€ 30** a year.

It is therefore advisable to do a search to compare your bank account with those on the market choosing the one that best suits you, even evaluating the options available at the post office.

THIS ADVICE WILL ALLOW YOU TO SAVE € 50 PER YEAR.

9. Save money on your free time

After having worked all week, having done physical activity, having suffered stress from external situations, we need to go out and get some fresh air, perhaps in the company of a friend or of our partner. On Saturday afternoons or evenings it is almost mandatory to go out and have fun, perhaps having a drink, taking a trip out of town, going to a club or having two beers in a pub. Unfortunately, even our free time considerably affects our wallets. Surely this type of expenses, compared to paying bills, are made lightly, and often we do not realize how much we actually spend for an evening with friends.

Certainly free time is just a moment to stop thinking and to have fun, but we could consider the idea that you can have fun even spending less or maybe not spending anything.

In winter it is a bit difficult to organize something that is not indoors, but even in this case you could do activities that you may never have considered. Bars and clubs cost, an evening at home with friends does not.

Possible Saturday afternoon and Saturday evening

activities are: go to city centre to have a drink with friends, this has an average cost of **€ 10**; cinema, for example, is another super popular activity of Saturday afternoon and has an average cost of **€ 10**. For dinner you can go to a fancy little place that will cost you about **€ 40** and finally an evening at the disco or in a place where to enter and / or have a drink you will spend about **€ 20**. Considering a Saturday afternoon-evening with all these activities we will spend about **€ 80**, but consider that all this is done every 15 days and not every week. The cost will be of **€ 160** monthly.

Now let's look at some activities that we could do instead without spending absolutely nothing. By checking the social networks or the websites of your favourite places, you can find some free or discounted events, that will allow you to do something new without spending much at the same time. For example, in summer it is very common to find concerts, festivals or fests that ensure fun and allow you to do something different from usual programs.

In winter the situation is a little more difficult, but even here the solutions can be found, for example organizing a cinema evening at home, buying only some crap for your friends, with a minimum expense of **€ 10**, or a dinner where you cook or everyone brings something to eat. In addition to this it is possible to search for events such as "Free Sundays at the Museum", book presentations in bookstores, to look for places where entry is free and where you have never been, for example an art gallery or a castle.

If you need to save money, even paying attention to how to distribute money during leisure time can help your pockets.

THIS ADVICE WILL ALLOW YOU TO SAVE FROM € 100 TO € 160 PER MONTH.

10. Save money on holiday

Travelling is one of the favourite pastimes of most people, of whom 84% book their holiday online. We all want to see new places, sometimes we want to escape from the situations that life presents to us, and in these moments what is better than leaving for a completely different place from where we live? Sometimes, on the other hand, you really need to take a break and indulge in a vacation, a rest from work, from the stress of the city, from what we have around us. Finally, there are those who travel for pleasure, because they simply love learning about new cultures, new places, new foods and new people.

Compared to the past, today it is much easier to move around and speaking about prices, these are much more accessible, not only to a privileged elite, but to everyone. Travel and vacation are no longer things for rich people. With globalization, travelling today is almost taken for granted in our lives, whether for work or vacation. People work and live in two different places, they move without problems and international borders hardly exist anymore.

It must be said that those who have economic problems easily give up going on holidays, because they certainly have more important expenses to deal with, but it is possible to go on an adventure even with little, there is no need to spend a lot of money, and it is also possible to book everything in advance just to pay less.

Today the low cost airlines offer many alternatives and the hostels or the AirB & b are an economic and excellent solution that replaces the expensive hotel. We often think that the hotel is more suitable, more furnished, more luxurious, but in reality there are magnificent places in which we can stay, as hostels or Bed & Breakfast.

We all deserve to admire the beauties of the world so if we want to go on vacation, we can try to find a cheap way to save some money in our pockets. Certainly, to save a little, we should also choose different destinations that still offer a special atmosphere, or we could simply book well in advance.

Let's take an example of a standard trip for a family of 4 people, 2 adults and 2 children (7-8 years), for 10 days in Sharm el Sheikh, in July, high season. Booking in May, about two months before, in a travel agency. So a typical situation for a normal family.

The package is made with a tour operator, and counting that children under 18 are free, the price is around € 3000, including an all-inclusive service in the tourist village, flight and accommodation. In addition there is the percentage that the travel agency takes of those € 3,000.

Now, however, the same family books the trip <u>from home</u> and instead of leaving in July decides to leave in September, before the school starts. Doing the necessary research on the internet, we can buy a flight for 2 adults and 2 children for about € 330.

The hotel must necessarily be on the coast because in Sharm el Sheikh there are no public accesses to the beaches, or we would also pay the access to the beaches so, to avoid this, we could rent an apartment in one of the tourist villages. Pay attention, this is very different from a hotel, even if it is located in a tourist village. You will have an apartment with all the comforts, with the access to the beach and the use of the swimming pool of the structure, without however having meals included. Booking a service this way will cost around **€ 360**.

Shopping or eating in a restaurant in a country like Egypt becomes very cheap as prices are really low.

The flight together with the apartment come in total **€ 690**. The rest of the € 3000 could be spent for the rest of the holiday, lunches, dinners, souvenirs and excursions between the sea and the desert.

THIS ADVICE WILL ALLOW YOU TO SAVE ABOUT € 2310 FOR A FAMILY HOLIDAY.[2]

---

[2] Prices have been accurately calculated on the Alpitour and on booking.com

11. Bring lunch from home to the office

The hectic life we do forces us to wander around all day and often stay away from home, having to eat meals elsewhere. In fact, we often do not even have time to have a lunch, for example, which allows us to give our body the right amount of energy, then eating whatever comes in front of us, because we find ourselves being too hungry. Our body needs the right sustenance and eating in an unbalanced way, not eating at all, or ingesting unhealthy foods will damage our body. So you should always have some snacks on hand or try to eat healthily.

Our work, which often has confusing schedules, forces us nearly every day to spend at least a lunch break in a restaurant or in a fast food restaurant. This happens especially to those who travel for work and are often forced to stop in roadside restaurants or in diners along the way to appease hunger and be able to continue to produce for our society.

Offices, for example, are equipped with vending machines for snacks, which are unhealthy and expensive for our pockets. Every day to dampen the hunger it is usual to take one of those snacks together with a coffee and then return to work immediately. An expense that includes a daily snack and a coffee can get us to spend about **€ 10** weekly (**€ 2 * 5** working days), for a total of **€ 40** monthly.

If instead you usually have lunch outside the office, going to the usual restaurant or to a fast food restaurant, you will spend on average **€ 5** a day, for a plate of pasta and a bottle of water and sometimes a side dish. This way, you can spend up to **€ 20** each week, always calculating 5 working days, for a total of **€ 80** a month.

Almost a hundred Euros of our salary to eat only for lunch every day, which is maybe a bit much. But as said above, here too there is a solution that we can put into practice bettering our condition.

The first thing to do is to draw up a small calendar, like the ones we did at school for schedules and subjects, writing down food to prepare and the day of the week to eat it. For example: Monday-pasta, Tuesday-salad, Wednesday-sushi and so on; now you have the plan of what you need to buy for the entire week. The second step is to go to the supermarket and buy the ingredients you need, ingredients that you will use to prepare more than one lunch.

For example, buying a pack of pasta (**€ 2**), a pack of

rice (**€ 2**), a tuft of salad (**€ 1**), seasonings and ingredients for your dishes like corn, cherry tomatoes, carrots, sauce, oil, salt and vinegar, mushrooms etc, you will spend a maximum of ten Euros, which is weekly expenditure of **€ 15** in total, and this will allow us to eat healthy and have a good lunch every day, even varying the diet, so to give the right nourishment to our body.

Always eating snacks, or always giving our body the same food, such as salad every day, is not good for our body and is not good for our wallet.

Let's save calories and money at the same time, keeping us fit!

THIS ADVICE WILL ALLOW YOU TO SAVE ABOUT € 20 PER MONTH.

12. Choose generic drugs instead of original ones

Health, as we have already repeated many times, is very important and should not be neglected. If you have serious problems, if you need to visit with specialist, the subject of saving must be left aside because, precisely, you must not neglect your organism or avoid being checked, for no reason. We are taking health as an example, however, in case of small problems and therefore the purchase of medicines for simple treatments. We should not neglect health for the fear of spending too much money, we should continue to make routine visits and take care of ourselves.

To save on health we can consider the idea of buying generic drugs and of going to the doctor to have them prescribed, as often some of them cost much less and what you pay is only the price of medical ticket. Just to see a practical example, a box of Gaviscon Advance normally costs **€ 4.95**, while going to the doctor and having it prescribed, we would only pay **€ 0.50**. A saving higher than **€ 4**. Many times we buy medicines without thinking that we could pay them less, simply by going to the doctor to get a recipe, which lasts six months (for "white" recipes) and allows us to save more. This, of course, applies to basic medicines, which everyone takes and do not refer to particularly serious diseases.

When the doctor prescribes specific medicines for a certain period and which are prescribed with a "pink" recipe, then we can think of buying generic drugs. It is usually the pharmacist himself who advises us the generic drug, to run the economy of drugs. The generic drug has the same effect of the branded one. The branded drug costs more simply because it is patented, it is a brand that has acquired fame and fame over the years. The active ingredients of the generic are the same of the branded drug.

Let's consider Tylenol, which is the classic medicine we take when we have taken a flu, which contains paracetamol. When the patent of Tylenol registered by the pharmaceutical company that produced it expired, other pharmaceutical companies hurried to produce the same medicine. An equivalent of Tylenol is **generic Paracetamol** whose price is **20-30%** lower than Tylenol.

The saving we have buying the generic drug instead of the brand-name one ranges from a minimum of around 7% to a maximum of over 40%, with an average of almost **23%**. These data were calculated on some of the best selling drugs that we can find in the table below.

Italian source: www.equivalente.it

ACTIVE INGREDIENT	BRANDED DRUG	DOSAGE	BRANDED PRICE	GENERIC PRICE	PRICE DIFFERENCE / %
PARACETAMOL	Tachipirina	16 cpr 500 mg	5,80 €	5,20 €	0,60 € (-10,34%)
	Efferalgan	16 cpr eff 500 mg	5,60 €	5,20 €	0,40 € (-6,9%)
NIMESULIDE	Aulin	30 doses 100 mg	4,43 €	2,60 €	1,83 € (-41,31%)
	Mesulid	30 doses 100 mg	4,43 €	2,60 €	1,83 € (-41,31%)
DICOFLENAC	Voltaren	30 cpr 50 mg	4,64 €	3,86 €	0,78 € (-16,81%)
	Voltaren	gel 50g 1%	6,90 €	6,20 €	0,70 € (-10,14%)

Consider buying all these medicines, but branded, because we do not believe in the effect of generic drugs or because this is what was recommended to us by the doctor, we would spend **€ 31.90**. While if we decide to buy the same drugs but trusting the generics, then our expense will be **€ 25.66**. Surely we will not save millions in this specific case, but doing the accounts well every time we buy a drug we will save **20-30%**.

THIS ADVICE WILL ALLOW YOU TO SAVE ABOUT € 6.00 FOR EVERY MEDICAL EXPENSE.

13. Avoid gambling

Often to try our luck we risk losing our money. Scratch and win, Slot machines, lottery, Bingo and more, are all games of chance that push us more consumers to try to make ends meet by winning maybe millions of euros with which we could feel satisfied and seemingly happy. We know well that happiness is not given by material goods, as the lifestyle teaches us by minimalists, and above all that it is not so easy to obtain it. It would be nice if we were happy only with a lottery ticket. One thing is trying your luck every now and then, investing a couple of euros, another one is doing it every day. Sometimes it also happens to win and to have luck, we are happy with this and again retry the winnings, investing even more money but doing so we do not realize that instead of earning we are losing money.

It is found that no one gives anything to anyone and that behind every game there is a trick. No winnings will ever be high enough to allow a lifetime without working, perhaps on an island while drinking fruit cocktails from morning to night. In case we win a large sum of money we should ask how much money we actually spent before we get this payout, how much time has passed before we got it and especially if we really needed it. In fact, we did not win, we returned to have the money we had before or at most we had a small gain, but it is never the figure that is actually written on the winning ticket. To have money for a project, to live a fulfilling life, to get to have a pension fund, to work and save, to make sacrifices. But above all spending money on something utopian like a lottery ticket is not necessary as you do the shopping and from this thought we begin to return to the goal that is saving. So gambling is superfluous in our lives and creates psychological dependence.

Let's consider a common person who spends **€2** every day for a scratch card or a lottery ticket. Monthly this person will spend **€60**.

Instead of playing every day and risk losing more and more money we put aside those two euros in a piggy bank, we would get a lot of savings at the end of the year, only accumulating money that we would have otherwise thrown. If the daily spending was higher at the end of the month we would have spent unnecessarily much money with which we could have done more important things like paying for example a bill. We always remember the lifestyle we talked about at the beginning of this booklet.

Maybe not everyone play or try their luck every day, but this advice serves to reflect on what seems an entrance but that is actually a loss for our heritage. It can be more profitable to invest money in shares, in an apartment, a company, which, despite being a risk, are more likely to increase our pockets instead of making us throw money. Then of course it depends on how lucky you are, you have to say that rarely happens, but there are people who often win at this type of game. You really have to have a lot of luck but it is always better to save than to lose a lot of money, remember.

THIS ADVICE WILL ALLOW TO SAVE FROM €60 UP PER MONTH.

14. Save money by Shopping Online

Now let's see, however, some suggestions regarding online shopping. Is it really worth buying items on the Internet? Shopping online today has become a regular action for more or less all. Who doesn't know **Amazon**?! A supermarket and online shopping mall that allows you to buy any product at an affordable price. The service is great, you expect the return and also the free shipping at times. But above all it is protected and in case of problems there is a good service center available.

This new way to buy merchandise is able to offer many advantages over traditional shops located in your own city. You can choose anything and save at the end of our spending. You can buy cosmetics, clothes, food, furniture, appliances and much more. A very expensive product in the shop can be found online at different internet sites with lower prices or on offer, so it is possible to buy with less effort and more carefree.

One of the most successful sectors which is online, where you can take advantage of excellent promotions, is that of **household appliances** and

Electronics products. In fact, in online shops you can buy televisions, mobile phones, audio systems, refrigerators, washing machines, ovens, dishwashers, etc. Of all these products you can also find a wide choice. Considering, for example, that a phone can cost even **€50** less than the store, many consumers now use this purchase method.

Buying this kind of products can scare you, first because you are afraid of a scam that will only fetch us money without receiving the product in exchange or selling it defective; second because there is the fear of not being able to manage and assemble very bulky equipment such as a washing machine or a television, moreover alone.

But you have to consider, in addition to saving, the idea that there are many reputable online stores, which have sold any type of product and appliance for many years, obtaining so in time trust from the customer. An example of online electronics store, become a colossus in the industry over the years, is **ePrice**. Here you can find any product you are looking for at low and affordable prices without fear of taking candles for lanterns.

We have to say about the second problem that online warehouses that sell this type of products, often have services such as **delivery and installation** of the appliance purchased.

When you purchase these products, as well as in the case of furniture, you can pay a small additional amount to obtain extra services, such as delivery to the floor, the installation of the product, the withdrawal of the old one and also the withdrawal of the packaging.

But now let's talk about the economic aspects. Is it really possible to save this way? Of course, it is! Especially if you pay attention to the offers and you take advantage of the **discount codes**. The latter are a great opportunity for the customer, because they are simple, free and can give us many discounts on purchases. Just visit a site of discount codes and look for the promotion that interests us, for example those active on appliances, or click on a promotion in particular. This way we can take advantage of a discount on the chosen product.

The reasons to buy on the internet are really a lot, starting from the great savings that you can get, the service at home and, when needed, the installation, and the comfort that this technology allows is not less important. We can shop online at any time of day, maybe during the breaks at work without wasting too much time leaving the house and going around to various shops, wasting fuel or money for parking.

Buying online allows you to save a lot of money. As an example, we could buy a very common washing machine in one of the shopping malls, like **Mediaworld**, at an average price of **€350**. Looking online we will realize that the average price of a washing machine, on an internet site specialized in household appliances, will be **€250**.

The money saved will not be only those on the appliance but also those on gasoline and especially on the time.
If then you want to be safer, then you can go to see the product first in a physical store, to touch it with your hand and decide on your purchase. This will make you feel more comfortable before entering our credit card numbers on the site under consideration. Good shopping!

This advice is going to allow you to save more than € 100.

THIS ADVICE WILL ALLOW YOU TO SAVE MORE THAN € 100.

15. Save money by optimizing the use of household appliances

After talking about buying appliances we are going to see how it is possible to save money when using them. We know that from their use at home comes a great part of our water and light bills of, so it would be great if we could know how to save using them. When we hear about energy saving, we must think that the concept also refers to our homes, to our small daily consumption, which multiplied by all users becomes a disproportionate consumption. In fact, about 36% of CO_2 emissions are due to residential consumption, a percentage that could be lowered considerably if the idea of energy saving is taken into account. Reducing home consumption can help to reach our goal, helping us to save money.

The houses of our territory until recently were not efficient and were not considered to be zero-impact, to date our government is adopting new forms of protection that will perhaps lead to an improvement of the condition of the air we breathe, thanks to new agreements with the countries of the European Union.

The money that an Italian family pays reaches quite

high figures that can be improved with small precautions. In the table below there is the average consumption and costs of household appliances of a typical Italian house. The light is included but in this case we do not consider it, we will talk better later.

Italian source: Lucegas.it

Appliance	Hours of Use /year	Power W	Consumption kWh/year	Cost €/year
Television	1.280 (4 hours a day)	150	190	35
Hair-dryer	160 (half an hour a day)	1800	290	53
DVD player	140	150	20	4
Laundry machine	260 cycles/year (5 kg of cotton linen at 60°)	Class A	240	44
Dishwasher	220 cycles/year (12 covers)	Class A	220	40
Fridge - Freezer	8760	Class A	305	56
Air conditioner	Fabbisogno freddo: 1300 kWh	COP: 3	425	78
Microwave oven	160 (half an hour a day)	1500	240	44
Electric oven	52	2000	105	20
Iron	160 (half an hour a day)	1000	160	30

Vacuum cleaner	104	1800	185	35
Computer	640 (2 hours a day)	150	95	15
Lightening	4800 living room, 3800 kitchen, 1900 rooms and bathroom	Fluorescent: 12	150	30
Total			**2625**	**483 €**

The first step is to check if all the household appliances we have in our house are necessary. It happens to buy or to receive for present an appliance that we hold there on the kitchen counter always on and that we do not use, for example a food processor. But it also happens that for laziness we buy appliances that we could do without, for example why not make the juice simply squeezing an orange on the juicer instead of using electricity? We are often lazy but we should try to eliminate the superfluous and to use only what we really need. It is not easy to quit to use dear appliances but if you want to save you need to sacrifice yourself. There is a rule in minimalist philosophy, to take an item that we haven't used for three months and ask ourselves if we would use it in the next three months. If not, then we can throw it away because it is superfluous.

FRIDGE: This appliance needs to remain on perpetually and above all it is part of the extremely necessary ones, especially when it is hot. So here we cannot just decide to unplug when no longer needed, but there is a way to save on the consumption of this appliance. which is to place the refrigerator in order to let it "breathe" and not crush it between the walls. Being too attached to the walls it will have to work twice to better cool the food inside. Also it would be better to avoid opening and closing the door continuously, so you will not have to work continuously to return to the right temperature. The fridge heats up immediately as soon as it is opened and therefore the energy to be produced is greater. Also the light inside that turns on and off consumes energy.

LAUNDRY MACHINE: The A+++ model is the one most suitable if we want a eco-friendly house. It is advisable to load it when the basket is full and washing the cloths always at low temperatures. Wash at 30 or even 40 degrees saves a lot per year compared to washes at 90 degrees; basically we would have a double saving.

Finally, it is useful to know that if we wash the cloths from 7 pm onwards the energy will cost less. The same tips can be used for the dishwasher.

ELECTRIC OVEN: Use the gas oven would be better,

although less comfortable, and it would allow an immediate saving, but it is possible to bring down the consumption even with the oven, following some tips like to avoid opening the oven continuously during cooking, do not heat the oven too early, it takes 5-10 minutes, try to keep the resistance clean and finally turn off the appliance a few minutes before the supposed cooking time of the food. The oven is hot and what we have in the oven will continue to bake.

COMPUTER AND TV: Activating the standby mode is useful to reduce the consumption of a PC, even if they are now programmed for energy saving. Disconnect the plug every time we stop using PC, printer, scanner, etc.

As for televisions nowadays technology has adapted them to energy saving and this already allows a great saving compared to old televisions. Try to disconnect the plug and check the standby mode is always better.

Following these little tips you can get to save about **10%** on the consumption of household appliances, which however constitutes about **80%** of our bills.

THIS ADVICE WILL ALLOW YOU TO SAVE ABOUT € 45,30 a YEAR.[3]

---

[3] The calculation was made considering the numbers in the table, eliminating electricity as had been said.

16. Use natural products to clean your home

The next tip is dedicated to household products and detergents, another commodity that occupies an important place in our monthly expenses. The detergents that we use are often predominantly composed of chemicals that damage our respiratory system or the skin, as well as the environment. Let's always remember to respect the place where we live and that we share with other living beings and organisms, our planet.

If the environment is not your first thought, remember that the chemicals with which we come into contact during cleaning are harmful in the long run, so it is good to put gloves and masks when you do the housework. There are several incidents due to chemical products that can occur with chemicals.

The home cleaning products we can't do without are:

- Dishwashing detergent (average cost €1.00);

- Dishwasher Gel or tablets (€10.00);

- Bleach (€1.00);

- Surface Cleaner (€4.00);

- Alcohol (€1.00);

- Anti-limestone (€2,00);

- Sanitizing tablets for Water (€1);

- Anti-dust spray (€1,50);

- Descaler for the wc (€2,00);

- Cloths detergent (€3.00);

- Fabric softener (€1.50);

- Soap of Marseille (€1.50);

TOTAL Monthly €32.50

To save on this spending the first advice is not to wait to do large cleaning but to clean a little at a time so as not to accumulate too much dust or too much dirt. Waiting too much time between one cleaning and the other you are risk to make even more effort and to use more product at once, just because the dirt has encrusted. It is not necessary to have many expensive products for the house, but also in this case we could use alternative solutions, perhaps using the good and old advices of our grandma. Salt, lemon, bicarbonate are all ingredients that we find in our kitchens and besides being ecological, they can help us in cleaning more than we think.

For the crockery, the floors and also for the laundry, the bleach can be replaced with a dear friend, **sodium percarbonate**, which is a natural whitening and is very economical (approximately **€1**), it is a stain remover for dirty laundry and it is great for bathroom and kitchen surfaces. To this you can add the **bicarbonate** to disinfect **(€0.50)**. Another useful product, in addition to seasoning dishes in the kitchen, is white vinegar **(€0.70)**. White vinegar can replace the glass detergent, the rinse aid of the dishwasher and it cleans the washing machine, such as anti-Calc. You can even mix the vinegar with some hot water and wash the floors. One last tip is to use the newspaper sheets to clean windows and mirrors. Maybe over time we have accumulated old newspapers that before being thrown away could be used for a final purpose. We must remember to cover our hands with gloves both because of the black ink that the newspaper will leave and because oil doesn't do very well to our skin.

By following these little tips you can save a lot and have a fresh and clean home.

THIS ADVICE WILL ALLOW YOU TO SAVE ABOUT €30.30 PER MONTH.

17. Avoid disposable tableware

Disposable products such as plastic plates and cups, paper napkins, disposable place mats, are very comfortable during dinners and birthday parties. They are often used when, on special occasions, we want to avoid washing many dishes or often because we are in a hurry and for convenience we avoid taking ceramic plates and then leave them dirty in the washbasin.

If we stopped using the disposable tableware we could save money and certainly improve the conditions of the environment, because these are not at all environmentally friendly. Even the same absorbent paper could be easily replaced with cotton cloths, which can then be washed in the washing machine with a tablespoon of bicarbonate.

We do not need to buy rags, we can recycle old sheets or old clothes by cropping them and, if we know how to do it, sewing them, creating colorful pieces to dry and clean our house.

We should eliminate the paper napkins using those of cloth as well as the disposable tablecloths, replacing them with real cotton tablecloths. Also for these there is the washing machine with bicarbonate, that will remove the stains along with a little vinegar.

If you don't like tablecloths you could adapt to the USA method, using plastic placers that can be rinsed with a sponge after each meal.

Regarding the dishes, cutlery and glasses it does not matter to use the good service, just take different crockery, the ones we have. The table will be more colorful and more welcoming. Imagine a dinner with friends or a family lunch, it would give a feeling of joy to the situation.

Do not be scared by the costs that could lead to wash the dishes, because a dishwasher consumes less than a hand wash. The plastic dishes are something superfluous, which damages the environment.

Let's see how much it costs to buy plastic crockery every month, to use them at every meal, considering we would need about 100 pieces.

- White plastic plates, 100 pieces €5.00 on average;

- Transparent plastic cups, 100 pieces €4.00;

- Set of plastic cutlery with napkin, 100 pieces €20;

As we can see the money that we spend on disposable plastic crockery could be spent on other things like the consumption of the dishwasher, that will be even lower, or to buy a full service of crockery; even this cost a lot less. Let's then use ceramic dishes and put them simply into the dishwasher.

THIS ADVICE WILL ALLOW YOU TO SAVE ABOUT €29 PER MONTH.

18. Save water and money

Saving water in the bathroom, kitchen and garden will reduce the amount of your bill and will take care of our planet. We all know that water is a precious commodity that cannot be renounced. Water is bearer of life and must be protected and therefore spared.

Saving water is crucial to avoid to waste it, because it is not an inexhaustible commodity as we might think, especially with the whole climate change situation. So it is important to learn how to reduce waste with small daily gestures.

Italy is one of the largest water consumers in the world, according to statistics. Each of us consumes on average **215 liters** of water per day, against the 2.5 that represent the quantity necessary for life. We must keep in mind that there are 1.4 billion people who do not have enough drinking water, without counting the billion that does not have safe water available and the 3.4 million of people who die because of diseases due to non-drinking water.

In particular, water is used for: discharge of baths, 8 liters approximately (**28%** of the consumption); personal hygiene such as bath, shower, teeth, hands

(**23%**); washing clothes, crockery and linen (**14%**); watering plants (**14%**); cooking (**13%**) and finally losses of hydraulic systems (**8%**). We waste so **78,475** liters, paying an average bill of **€420** per year. Prices are different depending on the region, Tuscany is the one where the water costs more, while Molise is the cheapest region.

So how can we make this expense less heavy? What are the actions you can put into practice to save money and save the planet at the same time? Let's see some trick to apply during the everyday life. The first trick is to **close the taps** while brushing your teeth or shaving (5 minutes a day), you can save **6 liters of water** per minute. Often we do not realize it, but since it flows out quickly the water goes away in a moment.

Even if we are used to bathing it would be better to **prefer the shower** and decrease the time of stay. Every minute you consume between 6 and 10 liters of water (10 minutes a day). Installing then ventilated taps you would cut the consumption half. A small addition would be to **collect the water from the shower** in a basin, while waiting for the hot water to escape, then use it to unload the toilet. If we have **water leaks** from the taps, then we should fix them. Leaking faucets cost **21,000 liters** a year. An exorbitant amount of water that without realizing it is thrown away in the void.

As we said some advice ago, it would be better to use the dishwasher and the washing machine fully loaded. This foresight will save about **8200 liters** of water per year.

When we have to thaw food, it would be better to do it in a basin, leave them under running water would waste **6 liters** per minute (5 minutes per day). Maybe it's not a daily action, but it affects our final bill.

Finally checking the water meter would be ideal to monitor our consumption, writing it down so that we can compare it with the bill.

But let's see all this turned into money.

Considering the advice listed above we could get to save about **59,000** liters of water per year, then consuming **19,170** liters. This will significantly drop the cost of our annual bill, paying just about **€96**.

The math should of course be done for each individual or household, as the bill changes for each user as well as for each region. Here the math was made on an average of costs recorded during national surveys, which allow to calculate the approximate figures. So, prices don't relate to every single consumer.

The advice is to monitor water consumption, before starting to save and after, to understand what the actual savings are. Let's not forget to add it all to our Excel table.

THIS ADVICE WILL ALLOW YOU TO SAVE ABOUT €320 PER YEAR.

19. Save your money buying used school books

Every year in September schools reopen and the university courses start again, and in this period both parents and pupils looks for school supplies and especially textbooks. The latter are a really exaggerated expense and the wallet pours tears throughout the purchase period.

A statistic, made by Italian **Federconsumatori** estimated an average cost of **€460** to a pupil who attends middle and high schools, while, according to another survey, a university student spends on average **€400** the year to buy textbooks.

Save money however is possible, using different ways instead of the classic stationery or bookstore, for example buying used books in markets, usually specialized markets are held every year in big cities between September and October. It is true that the market today are less diffused than in past years, but this happened only because technology is overcoming more and more borders, even, and perhaps above all, in publishing. This e-book is the example. Despite this, there are several ways to save money and you just have to do some foresight and know how to use well the Web.

According to a survey from Skuola.net, most Italian families (**64%**) prefer to buy new textbooks, because the books are often updated and then you should still add extra information, but also because used books are underlined or perhaps written. However, from the figures we can see that buying new books leads to a major expense that could be definitely halved.

So, if we do not love to buy used books, we could opt to buy them online or in our preferred supermarket. Books online stores in recent years are catching on thanks to the convenience of receiving books directly at home and especially because these are discounted on the cover prices, discounts that are not applied in library.

The easiest platform where is possible to buy textbooks is definitely **Amazon**, which as we well know is the number one e-commerce. Buying schoolbooks on Amazon is very easy, just go to the "***Back to school***" section or simply enter the title or author in the search area. This also applies to university books, often discounted or at significantly lower prices. If you make a wrong order Amazon allows you to send back the goods and send you a voucher in return, so you can repeat the operation. In addition, the section "*Back to School*" allows you to access the list of schoolbooks that you need without having to enter directly the title of the books. Finally, if the amount is greater than **€60**, you are entitled to a discount coupon in the school sector.

Going back to used books, if you do not have time to go around markets, you can take a look to Libraccio.it, an e-commerce specialized in the sale of second-hand books, chosen specifically for their quality. So, these will not have missing covers or pages, they of course have signs of wear, underscores and notes but will be suitable to be used again. On the site you can also buy new books and in case take advantage of discounts that e-commerce makes available for new customers.

Speaking about those who are unfamiliar with computers or online buying, or maybe those who do not trust much these new technologies. In this case we can go to big malls or supermarkets like **Carrefour, Coop, Auchan, Conad, Esselunga, Simply** and **Pam Panorama** and ask to buy the schoolbooks. By doing so we will get books at discounted prices and coupons to use in the store on all school supplies.

Buying books Online or in a supermarket you can save from **15** to **20%** on the expense that we usually do every year, spending on average **€380** instead of

€460. If we buy the textbooks online, it is worth noting that we would also save on the gasoline that we will need to move from home and on time.

THIS ADVICE WILL ALLOW YOU TO SAVE FROM €70 TO €100 PER YEAR.

20. Save your money reading online newspapers

The daily newspaper, a faithful companion during those short pauses of relax that we take to detach from the hectic day due to work commitments, family and problems of the moment. The newspaper, with all those little black and white letters and advertisements for promotions and products, updates us daily on the events of the world. It is usually used by those who are never at home are not able to see the news on TV, but also from those who have used it for years. If we go to a bar many people sip a coffee while they are you mean to read the news in the local newspaper or on the "*Gazzetta dello Sport*". There are those who then among their habits have that of buying the newspaper just left the house, before going to work, or who are subscribers and receives it directly at home in the morning.

This little moment of relaxation and information is going to affect our wallet, and a bit like coffee in the morning could make us lose some useful savings for a project or for a savings fund.

A daily newspaper in Italy costs on average **€1.30**, this means that monthly we would spend about **€40**. This money may seem little, but accumulated will make a high amount of money, almost as much as that of coffee at the bar. If our goal is saving, then it is clear that maybe buying the newspaper every morning could be a luxury to be no longer allowed. But this does not mean that we can no longer follow the news or that we can no longer indulge in moments of relaxation during the day as once. Today the Web offers many alternatives and among these there are also online newspapers. There are so many sites on which you can follow news, on which you can read what happened in the world while you were seeing your lives.

We could read the newspaper everywhere, even during our coffee breaks, through our smartphone or as we are doing now reading this ebook. Nowadays almost all of us are equipped with laptops and we all have a mobile phone that allows us to go on the Internet, offers for Giga consumption are cheaper and cheaper. Moreover you don't need to go on the internet, but you can read your favorite newspapers or keep in touch with what happens in the world, like the situation of the stock exchange, sports and much more, downloading apps from the store of your operating system. Some of these are <u>ansa.it</u>, TGcom24, *"Gazzetta dello Sport"*, Il Giornale.

With these apps we can keep in touch with reality without having to spend a Euro, staying up to date on our favorite team, reading interesting articles and learning new things.

Another completely free way to read the news and to be aware of what happens around us, are the social. Every newspapers listed above has a Facebook page and update its bulletin board with new news every day.

For more curious people and for those who want to learn or improve a new language, there is also an app, created directly by the BBC, with which to learn English while listening to the news of the day.

In conclusion we can see that even without the paper we can continue to learn news and to document us while we have a break during the day.

THIS ADVICE WILL ALLOW YOU TO SAVE €40 PER MONTH.

21. Save your money on Christmas presents

Perhaps the first thought that might come reading the title of this chapter is to not want to save on gifts, as it would seem a bad deed for the recipient, but it is absolutely not so. We must see the action to save on gifts as a gesture to be able to succeed in our intent, and above all we must think that the gift we are going to do in order to save money is not equal to the love that we want to show but that it symbolizes this love. You don't have to make expensive gifts to show that you love someone, but you need to do them lovingly. They are just a symbol, a through between us and those who receive the gift. We do not have to worry if someone will think that the gift is not at its height, that is not quite expensive or similar things, because it is not on this base that you evaluate the relationship between two people. Our friend who will receive the gift will understand that our gift is a symbol of affection, especially if it is done with our hands. An object produced by us is the symbol of what we want to convey to another person. These notions are valid all year round and not only at Christmas.

Every Christmas in the world **25 billion dollars** are

spent for gifts, which are often not appreciated. A huge amount with which we could really do much more, such as something that could help others, that would be a nice Christmas present. Often in the choice of the gift we are not very careful and this leads to a waste, the gift itself and the money with which we buy it. The race to presents is a period of fire and stress for each of us, especially in the last days preceding Christmas.

The gifts that every year we try to buy cost to each of us **€165** on average, according to data from *Confcommercio*. An important amount of money, since it is spent in just less than a month, sometimes in a week. Let's see what precautions can be put into practice to avoid a waste of Christmas gifts.

The list is always there each time we have to organize something. The list of people to which we must buy a gift and what items to buy these people, for example, can be a good start. Purchases in the dark confuse and tend to make you spending more money.

After making our list, instead of slingshot headlong between the streets, traffic and crowded shops, let's look at the e-commerce sites. These offer many products at very low prices compared to the store. By buying our gifts online, we could save **10** to **20%**.

Another advice is to give away something you can share, for example to couples of friends, families, avoid making individual gifts for each member of the nucleus, for example, you can offer a Christmas basket with food, sweets and drinks. This will save a lot of money compared to what it would entail to make a single gift for every single person. It often happens to us to not like a gift received, so let's not be ashamed and recycle it. If it is in good condition and it has never been used there is nothing wrong with giving it to someone else.

An idea for the most creative people is to make DIY gifts, designing with your own hands what then will be the present for the person you love. Building a handmade gift will cost almost nothing, if not the material that must be purchased, saving at least a **50%** compared to a gift bought.

If instead we are not creative people then we could opt for fair trade. At the Christmas markets or even in special shops you can buy these products that, in addition to having a reasonable price, will allow us to commit a good deed.

Finally remember to do not throw the receipts, this will allow us to make a budget and see how much we have really spent and maybe how we can improve even more the following year.

Coming to the practical aspect, of course this will depend on which way we choose to follow and the items we decide to buy. What we can say however, is that there will be a net savings compared to previous Christmases, at least a **20%**, which on balance will be **€132** instead of **€165**.

Deciding to shop online, instead of fight with an angry crowd in shopping malls and shops, then we will save a **10-15%** and spend about **€140**.

Opting for do-it-yourself then the prices are lowered considerably by a good **50%**, thus spending about **€80** for all our friends and relatives. The idea of spending hours creating objects is much more tempting than running around in the crowd to buy gifts at the last minute.

Finally, as the last advice of this chapter, we should try not to stress ourselves and make purchases calmly. You don't have to run or postpone your expenses to the last minute, but you just need to organize yourself in time.

THIS ADVICE WILL ALLOW YOU TO SAVE FROM €30 TO €80 EVERY CHRISTMAS.

22. Grow food on your balcony or in an urban garden

Previously we dealt with how to do the shopping, listing some tips and precautions to save money. What if, besides saving money, we try to cultivate some products in our house? There are lucky people who already have a garden, or a large space that will allow them to plant trees or plants more imposing than those who have only a balcony, but let's see which plants we can accommodate in our homes even if we have not much space. In addition to this we will also see later how we can have a small vegetable garden without owning a real garden.

Among the items we buy the most in the supermarket there are vegetables, fruits and vegetables, and sometimes also spices and aromatic plants, which we use to flavour our foods. Cultivating some of these products we would have a substantial savings on our expenses. It is not necessary to have a vegetable garden, it is enough to get some pots with Earth and a place them in the sun, because any plant, fruit or vegetable we decide to cultivate needs a lot of light. The soil can be made by mixing ground and animal manure or by a good compost already fertilized, purchased in the shopping malls dedicated to this hobby. After we have prepared the Earth in the pots we begin with the sowing, that can be done by transplanting an acquired sapling, or placing the seeds in the ground, waiting for the seedling to be born from the beginning. As for the seeds or the plants to buy remember that you have little space, so you should buy vegetables and fruits that are not too bulky such as tomatoes, mint, basil, rosemary, peas, parsley, valerian, broccoli and chicory. After having checked that everything is ready you will only need water to watering your plants (you could use rainwater so as not to use the house one, picking it up in basins) and lots of patience.

Having a garden at home, whether it is large or small, give a really important hand to our savings plan, even if the plants we cultivate are few, they however are products that we will not buy at the supermarket, where the fruit and vegetables have outrageous prices per kilo. The exact saving depends on what products you are used to buy and from which you decide to cultivate at home, but no matter what this will bring several pennies in your pockets.

Certainly also in this case we have to do some expenses, but they are really insignificant, the seeds for planting cost very little (**€ 1-2**), the land (the price of sacks starts from **€2**), and then the water, which as we have already said must not necessarily be consumed because you can collect that rainwater to water your plants.

Having a plot of land would be even more convenient, but if we live in a city we have to settle with the pots that we have on the balcony or, if you have the possibility, to cultivate in the gardens that some cities make available to the inhabitants. In order to become part of an **urban garden** you have to contact your municipality. The urban garden is a green space belonging to the municipality and is made available to citizens to cultivate fruits, vegetables and flowers. This initiative is useful to the society and to the economy of the citizens, a small space of 20 meters is able to produce fruit and vegetables for the support of a person for a period of one year. This really saves a lot both to a single person but also to a family of more than two people. These urban gardens are rising sharply because they also give to citizens who cultivate them a way to live a healthier life and to be in contact with nature. Usually, in fact, they are spaces that are outside the city walls, in the suburbs, where smog levels are reduced just to foster a healthier lifestyle. To be part of it you have to face the expense of a **small annual fee**, decided by your **municipality**. It is an annual fee but it will save quite a lot of money.

Finally, who is in constant contact with nature lives better, relaxes more. Living near a green area or visiting a lawn, garden or any natural space makes people happier. Moreover, it is to be said that material contact with nature, so gardening, take care of your plants, gives you satisfaction and harmony. Today our life is hectic and very stressful, the levels of sadness, nervousness and depression are always higher then to do gardening, even only on the balcony of your apartment, could be a way to carve out a moment of calm and serenity from your days, even if we dedicate yourselves to it only the weekend. So this beautiful project to cultivate the earth will bring a great success in your lives, both to save your money and to make your mind and your physique feel better. Think about the satisfaction of being able to eat a fruit cultivated in your land and with your hands.

The savings will depend on which of the two solutions you choose and how many and which plants you decide to cultivate. With an urban garden or a homemade vegetable garden you will save a lot more than planting spices and tomatoes in a pot on the balcony, but slowly you can reach a great goal.

Just consider that buying fruit and vegetables in the envelope, already cleaned and cut, an average family spends about **€2080** a year, while buying loose fruits and vegetables you can arrive to spend **€650** a year. By cultivating a vegetable garden or a small backyard you would spend about half of the last option, or about **€325** or so. There is always to consider which vegetables and what fruit you have in our garden.

THIS ADVICE WILL ALLOW YOU TO SAVE ABOUT €300 a YEAR.

23. Stop Ironing

Ironing is one of the most tedious things to do at home and the more you approach the beautiful days and the summer, the more tiring it becomes. In addition, this small household appliance consumes a lot of electricity at home.

Stop ironing and getting an impeccably folded and fit laundry, without using electricity and saving a lot of time, is possible. You just have to follow a small guideline:

- Use brief washing machine times;

- After rinsing, immediately hang up the clothes;

- Regarding the shirts, it is good to pull the fabric by hand after having washed them and let them dry on a crutch so as not to create cracks;

- Beat the towels and put them lying on the cloth.

An iron uses from **800** to **2000 Watts** per hour, it is possible to measure those used by our unit with a wattmeter, inserting it into the electric socket to which the iron is to be connected. But by doing a count here and assuming that on average an iron consumes **1100 W** per hour, or **1,1kWh**, and that the energy costs about **€0.45/kWh**, we will spend about €0.50 in one hour. Whereas on average we iron three times a week for a couple of hours, we spend monthly about **€15**.

This money seems insignificant, as we have also seen for other consumption. But accumulating these **€15** can allow you to save a lot. There is also to say that ironing useless, so it's all money that we could save. To disinfect the clothes that we wash we can use baking soda and vinegar, we do not need steam, as we saw when we talked about the products for home. In this way we can save time, energy and money.

THIS ADVICE WILL ALLOW YOU TO SAVE €15 PER MONTH.

24. Remove your landline

The landline has been part of our lives for decades, until the technological evolution has put it aside, even if not totally, to give space to the mobile phone, first and to the smartphones, then. The more technology evolves, the more old wheel phones are just a memory. Today we can do well without a landline, also because its costs are not light even if there is a lot of operators and promotions.

Let's remember our path to saving that requires us almost to eliminate the superfluous and nowadays the landline is just a piece of antiques. The costs of having a landline are full of extra payments, such as the monthly fee, the activation contribution, an eventual deactivation of the line and the activation, which together can get you to reach the **€100**.

It is important to note that there are offers that include ADSL but not calls, or the latter are paid through the connection fee, for example. These are more convenient, if you decide not to use the phone to call; at the way many other offers made available by different operators are more convenient. you must understand then which you think is the most convenient and which is right for your consumption.

Nowadays we use smartphones or Skype for calls, and consequently the landline can be deleted from your monthly expenses, choosing an offer that gives you only internet connection if you need it in the house and the smartphone is not enough. The offers that only include an internet connection will be like having the ADSL, only without wires around home. Certainly you must pay attention to the offers, and always noting the quality and not the quantity.

Offers without phone calls which include only the Internet are the best, they allow you to save obtaining, during the year, one or two monthly salary free.

To date, we do not make a lot of phone call since the social allow chat, audio messages and video calls only using the Internet.

Finally there is to debunk the myth that to have an ADSL in the house you need a landline. It is not so, now mobile rates include several GB of monthly traffic. For example 10GB of monthly data traffic are enough to browse online, watch movies or whatever.

On average an Italian with a landline spends monthly **€40** BETWEEN calls and ADSL, while if you purchase only Internet packages, you would spend on average **€20**, based obviously on how many GB you choose to use, or on the offer provided by the company. In short, you can save a good **50%**.

THIS ADVICE WILL ALLOW YOU TO SAVE €20 PER MONTH.

25. Save on light and gas bills, reading tips

Here we are, we have come to the last chapter of this first book on personal finance and as an advice to conclude this long list we will talk about bills of light and gas. We have seen water above and it is better not to torture ourselves too much as we have come to conclusions. The bills, those letters that every time, looking in the mailbox, we hope not to find and that we are afraid to open. Yes, because these are really what goes to send our bank account into a river of tears. Use of technology, computers, televisions, stereos, use of appliances and, above all, use of the bulbs, is the cost with the higher weight on our pockets and what forces us to limit ourselves in other areas of life, because of the risk of not being able to pay them. But we can also make sure to save on these, if reading them carefully you realize your real consumption.

First of all, let's start from reading the bills, try to understand the real consumption and what you really are going to pay.

The bill remains, in the eyes of the consumer, indecipherable, despite the companies of light and gas try to make it as transparent as possible. Being able to read the bill gives us a clearer view of our consumption.

The first information we find on the bill reminds us if we are part of the free **market** or we are in the most protected. Below we find the data **related to type of contract**, which is the features of the supply, for example the power of the meter and what is the supply that we have (e.g. maid).

The **Technical Information** section shows the codes that indicate our supply as the **POD** and the **PDR**, related to light and gas. Near the issuing date and the amount we can find the amount to be paid and the deadline within which must be paid. Below are reported the **Contact Details** to call in case of complaint or information.

The **total** bill is divided into four subheadings:

- Costs on **energy or natural gas**, in which the energy and gas prices applied to consumption are present;

- Cost of **transport and management of the counter**: These costs are related to the transport of energy from the power plants to the houses, also including the expenses for reading and maintenance of the counters. These are costs that all pay apart from the vendor.

- Expense for **system charges**. This item covers all the expenses that are used to keep the electrical and gas service in balance.

- The **RAI fee**, which is present in the bills of those who have a television. After this, we can find information about the **Meter Readings**. These readings are made by the customer and not by the supplier and are said, in fact, self-service readings. If the readings are estimated, it is worth to be careful if these will be subject to adjustment. Now let's talk about **detail elements**. These are the unit prices and the consumption to which the costs are applied. These will be available according to the type of contract.

- If you have an energy supply on the protected market, need to apply to the supplier;

- If instead you are part of the free market, you must check the contract with the supplier;

- If you present a complaint about an invoice or a request for a correction, this information must always be sent by mail. In Italy, electricity and gas bills are the most Expensive in Europe. Each family spends 15% more than the European average. According to the data, estimated by **Facile.it**, if in Italy the average European rates were applied, the cost of the bills would lighten by about **€240** per year.

Starting from the electricity bill, considering the average consumption of a family of about **2700 KWh** and a power of **3kW**, the electricity bill will cost **€537** per year. As for the gas bill, always considering an average consumption of an Italian family, or **1400 m³** by year, the cost will be about **€1050 per** year. The first rule to save on your bills is to consume as little energy as possible. You can observe a series of small tips, which in addition to reducing the consumption of light and gas in your home, would lower it globally, contributing to a more sustainable model. If every family user were to observe these small rules, the bill could come down by several Euros. Let's see what these precautions are:

- Turn off the lights in the empty rooms;

- Use the dehumidification mode of the air conditioner lowers the perceived heat;

- Adjust the water heater to 40 °C in summer and 60 ° C in winter, and turn it on only when needed;

- Set the temperature of the washing machine to 30 °C, and use the ECO function;

- Perform the washing of cloths and crockery at **full load**;

- Clean the air conditioner filters regularly;

- Close the fridge well and do not put hot food in it.

- Do not leave the apparatus in stand-by, for example using an electricity socket with a switch;

- Close the shutters in summer on very hot days and in winter at sunset;

- In winter, keep heating at a **temperature of 20 °C**;

- Do not cover radiators with panels or curtains;
- At night close well shutters or dampers;
- Make sure that no air passes through doors and windows.

You have also to pay attention to time slots. The meter that we mostly find in the Italian homes, allows to measure the electricity in the different time slots of consumption (monohourly, bihourly and triclockwise). Both in the free market and in the protected market, during the evening hours in the F3 slot, you have a lower price of energy. It is possible to obtain a small saving in the bill, orienting our consumption towards this time zone, as far as it is possible. For example, we can start the washing machine and the dishwasher late at night or in the morning before seven o'clock.

Finally, you should try to choose a light and gas offer more convenient than the one you use. The free market always offers affordable prices.

A great way to save on energy is to improve energy efficiency, both in plants and in household appliances. Some tips that you can implement are:

- Use energy-saving LED lamps;

- Buy class A appliances;

- Do not use a boiler;

- Install thermostatic valves;

- Replace the fixtures with insulating thermal cut models;

- Improve the thermal insulation of the walls and the roof.

All these precautions will save up to **50%** on gas and light consumption.

THIS ADVICE WILL ALLOW YOU TO SAVE €268.50 ON THE ELECTRICITY AND €525 ON THE GAS PER YEAR.

Another way to save money on gas and electricity costs is the **Energy Bonus** introduced by the Italian Government in 2007. This bonus is intended for the less rich users. You have to apply to have it and it allows you to save considerably on bills. The bureaucratic process is complex, but this advice can be adopted by those who are not economically enabled to make all those changes listed above, to make a home warmer and cheaper. The discount in the bill on the energy bonus is variable. The bonus is **€125** yearly for families composed of 1 to 2 people, **€153** If the family includes up to 4 individuals and, finally, **€184** If the household is even more numerous. Paying a bill from **€412** to **€354** per year. The gas bonus instead goes from a minimum of **€34** the year to **€273**, spending from **€2016** to **€1777**.

It can apply to any household that has the requirements of economic hardship, submitting the application to the municipality of residence or to centre for fiscal assistance, attaching the ISEE form and other necessary information.

THIS ADVICE WILL ALLOW YOU TO SAVE FROM €125 TO €184 ON THE COSTS OF ELECTRICITY, AND FROM €34 TO €273 ON GAS COSTS.

Conclusion

We arrived at the end of the long list of our tips on how to save and keep our Money Management under control. Following these 25 tips you can now start your journey towards safeguarding our heritage and the best management of our daily lives. The advices are obviously based on the generic habits of an average Italian person. The daily routine can't be the same for everyone, each of us uses to do different actions and programs, so the topics covered relate to the more generic lifestyle of a person in Italy.

In fact, in addition to those situations that we talked about earlier, there are several other ways to be able to put your money aside; This depends on what is your point of arrival, from your willpower, on the importance that has for you this path towards savings and Money Management.

Summarizing the advices expressed and the various possible situations, we can say that savings start from the moment we have breakfast, eliminating the appointment with the bar. The second important moment, that of lunch, instead can save us thanks to a nice packed lunch, prepared with our hands, during the work break. This new daily habit will bring you to live more healthily and can give you more time for you. There are also offices that offer employees relaxation or meditation rooms to use while enjoying lunch or just before starting work again.

Often the time frame to be used for sports in the morning is not long enough, so we often tend to go jogging or running, after we have finished working, but it would be better for the organism to do physical activity in the morning before we start our day. The body burns the fats of the previous day, while in the evening it will do a bier effort and will only burn the fats taken during the day. Following the advice given regarding not going to the gym, using the one we have at home, let's try to find a moment of the day that is before going to work.

The day continues and our wallet could easily be emptied because of a packet of cigarettes, a scratch card or an extra that would be better not to be allowed.

Let 's always stand before your goal and take care to note all our expenses, keeping the receipts. Try to be more autonomous from industrialization and try to create products for home, to cultivate fruits and vegetables in your garden and we aim straight to the goal.

This is not a lifestyle or health manual but let us remember that the economic aspect of our life is firmly linked to how we live it. If we adopt a minimalist lifestyle we will learn to save and optimize our lives and all aspects of it, including money. At the end of our journey we would have really saved a lot and this will make us happy and satisfied. And if you're afraid of changing habits, your own routines, your own ways of doing something, then you just need a little courage. Change is not a negative event, but it is something that will lead us to make a revolution in our lives. Think of change as a new beginning to live a more peaceful life, with more money that will allow us to realize what we have always wanted.

THANK YOU FOR PURCHASING THIS TIMELESS BUSINESS AND INVESTMENT MASTERPIECE – THE MONEY MASTERY TEACHER SERIES

Money Mastery Teacher provides "investment advice" services that are understandable, transparent and comprehensible. The focus of our content is on the domestic economy, asset management, and advanced investment. The content is inspired by a sincere approach to people, as well as the pursuit of optimal service and the greatest possible satisfaction.

We do not try to sell you theoretical information. Rather, we have worked out tailor-made solutions for you. Because we are not obligated to any other than you, and our high demands on ourselves.

We want to offer you a clever alternative to the domestic economy and advanced investment strategies. The highlighted business model is deliberately set up so that you can work detached from the conventional inside-the-box investment orientation. Thus ensuring that you are provided with the optimal solutions as you read through the pages of our books knowing fully well that each selection of financial approach is based on well-founded analysis and continuous quality controls.

Here at **Money Mastery Teacher,** we are committed to bringing you specialized domestic economics and advanced investment solutions through every single book that we publish.

I look forward to hearing your testimonies and awesome feedbacks. **Cheers!!**

Made in the USA
Columbia, SC
03 November 2019